PLASTIC TUBED LITT

Wendy Allen's work has appeared in *Poetry Wales, Ambit, The Moth, Banshee, Poetry Ireland Review, The North* and *Propel. Plastic Tubed Little Bird* is her debut pamphlet.

Also by Wendy Allen

The Tricolore Textbook   (Legitimate Snack, 2021)

Plastic Tubed Little Bird

Wendy Allen

Broken Sleep Books

ISBN: 978-1-915760-13-5

Cover designed by Aaron Kent

Edited & Typeset by Aaron Kent

Broken Sleep Books Ltd   Broken Sleep Books Ltd
Rhydwen   Fair View
Talgarreg   St Georges Road
Ceredigion   Cornwall
SA44 4HB   PL26 7YH

For Becca

Contents

Pelagos

After Barbara Hepworth

What happens when I look from the side
when I can't see the strings completely —
does that mean the sea disappears?

It is *Pelagos* I always go to first
at *The Hepworth*. From the front,
the repeat, the shadows, the stitches

transform my vulva into a perfect
circle as you reach around my waist,
from the side repeat, trace finger on back.

I hear a moan from the centre (my voice)
your cock is between my lips
I am the opposite to hollow now

the stitches are laced with immediacy
they mimic breathing
they rise - pause - fall

I move to the side, hold my breath
the sea stops moving -
land locked, absent body. In the gallery

we meet at cat's cradle
we begin on an elm flat base
lick salt off plate, off body

into the space, fold shouldered waves into me
sea wall curves over arms -
wrap around, repeat

I look at *Pelagos* from the side
I think of myself
open mouthed

an empty estuary
the size of an unspecified sea,
downy breathing

I'm almost complete in this part.
I am *Pelagos*. From the side
from the side, make my strings dissipate.

Plastic Tubed Little Bird

I hide the tampon within my fingers
like I'm holding a tiny, fragile bird.
Someone once told me this is how
my hands should be when I run.

On the side of an unstained trainer's edge
is a star. In red. On the edge.
I think of the tiny celestial mark I draw
in ink on my calendar, always inconspicuous.

I pretend to look for my phone, pen, a date
two weeks later. Inside my bag, a yellow wrapper
the colour of cruel. A creased spring dress
worn only to celebrate bloodshed.

I whisper period to you
in the hope you will turn around.
You don't, I shout it out
28 times aloud in my head.

When I empty my mooncup, the blood
remains crescent lonely in the daytime bowl.
I like the absolute discomfort
this causes you.

I envy the plastic backed sanitary sleeping
bodies on their unfamiliar coastal beds,
their one-night stand leaving them free
for me to feel their single use guilt.

A naked tampon in the cervix of my bag
is exposed only by a useless string lifeline,
the wrapper from the orange tampon
flatlines at the bottom of my bag.

You Wear a T Shirt with the National Rail Emblem on

From Chester to Bangor
the carriages peer
down on top
of the wide-eyed sea wall

you trace your two fingers slow
down the curve of my waist
to hipbone, to the sea underneath

you go down on me
your slated lips taste of waves
I am between blue and breathing.

Vade Mecum

(You Post the Doris Lessing Book to me)

I love you when you reply to my email with urgency — you write
in the exact way I remembered you speak — I picture your fingers
moving quickly over the keyboard — wish they were finding my
clitoris instead — that time your hand was under my skirt at the end
of term in '96 — you left too quickly — I used to watch you dance
to Cerys Matthews — planning what I would say — each time
rehearsing my soliloquy — each time spoken in silence — each time
hot faced with concentration — just saying goodbye in my head

Afterwards I read the book you send to me — in a film we'd know
it wasn't the Doris Lessing novel with your writing inside that made
the scene — it is the unwritten stage directions — the unseen asides
— the way you say oral — me fantasising — you licking me out in
the middle of the day — the way you look at me intensely — wishing
you were fucking me tenderly — you are the urgency I masturbate
with over the bath — always when the sun is high — I think of the
perfect shadow we would make

Why do People Take Photographs of Men Surfing and not my Orgasm as it Peaks

We are speechless
floating on our mattress of foam off the shore

my nipples are blushed buoys
as they bob on the slowing wave of you

my hair advert pretty as it moves
over your cock like the tide

I like the off white of afterwards,
dirty bridal stains traced on our lips

I want to stay open-mouthed,
remain on this high, photographed

on this invisible wave.
I want to have it framed —

do I smile as your tongue
turns circles into crests as I surface

The Tide Comes in Flat

I turn the blue estuary ruby
as you watch me
from your writing shed

the water is peony up close
a mix of blood clots like jelly fish
and semen crests, red edged

I heat the water on impact
which sets the blood permanently
on the inside of my thighs

you wrap a wool cardigan bandage
onto the wrong part of me
with hands that don't understand

Day 3

The poem is sex red gloss on my fingertip
when I fuck you against the hard wall.

It bleeds onto your iron-coloured shirt
when I ride your mouth. It tastes ripe

like July. When you lie back on the pillow
with that look that is post fuck slow,

it's the *Vaseline* like sheen on your lips
that thrills me. Metallic edged from biting,

it's a milk blush memory on the sheet underneath
that stains even after washing.

The Pink Roll Top Bath

I grasp a piece of invisible text from *Delta of Venus*
and bite so hard juice runs down
to where I'm smooth inside.
I am falling over the edge

in anticipation of your mouth.
My lips curve like the rim of the roll top bath,
they smile, then say,
fuck me over the side.

Open mouthed, soft inside, I swell,
clitoral bulbs freeze framed in slow,
they grow - lento. I'm an Attenborough nature programme,
my clitoris evolves from want.

Hot Priest

Through a veil we kiss	hot priest
we're together under this same sheet	hot priest
you don't look away	hot priest
you look at me	hot priest
I'm your deity	hot priest
the sheet a voyeur	hot
I'm wearing lipstick	hot
the exact colour of my cervix	hot
the purple of your cock	hot
rises again	hot
we match internally	hot
we kiss for eternity	hot
you love me despite	hot
the sheet yellows with time	hot
the sheet wears out	hot
I taste of garlic	hot priest
you lick my clitoris	oh so hot priest
the sheet is a confined space	hot
my nipples little tent pegs	hot
under this frayed embrace we kiss	hot
desire heightens under cover	hot
a pearl effect on the sheet	hot
that stiffens	hot
you kiss me despite	hot priest
oh god this is good	*oh my god hot priest*
your eyes wrap around my waist	hot priest
you're everywhere	priest
I taste you everywhere	hot hot priest
the sheet dissipates	priest
absolved	love does this

Barbara

The curve of the sculpture I look at in your garden makes the plate I eat off later appear square, I compare it to how you would have made it. Your curves are laced intricately, woven with the asides of being a woman, desire tied into the hard steel fixings, the smooth part of hip liquid yet solid under each gaze. You would have made this grey plate search for the intimate, holding a baby, the plate would still be tender even when empty. You would have made the plate, smoked a cigarette, your fingers tracing spaces in the air as you observe your circle turning square.

Mudlarking

What I looked like under the shallows

Only the dredged part of me remains.
It smells like the end.
This period is slow like sediment
and meanders instead of flows,
bleeds like shit and sticks
to the depths of the shallows.
This is the bottom of a coffee,
a slow draining punishment,
the dull lack left at the end.
The lustrous first blood has gone,
swimming red ribbon sleek
in a costume that dyes
the departing waters
like a menstrual bath bomb.
No cider black starburst
bleeds into the clean.
The clot at the bottom is dead brown,
a pencil end, a stub, a dry felt tip.

The night after the visit to the Sculpture Garden, July 1996

The smooth arch of arse cupped as he licks your clit.
Through cat's cradle I kiss him goodnight,
his tongue on rung, rubs me, loves me.
Dark iris, drown in blue grey. Through net of nerves
insert, criss crossed, barbed wire demarcation.
I'm safe in the curve of his arm, crawl out of messy

Shared Space

We share this same grey, and I like this. I fuck you against the doorframe while the shadows watch. Can't seem to stop. Today is Wednesday, a grey Monday impersonator. I want to curl up in your wool blanket. Can't seem to stop thinking about this. Shadows disappear, now we share the grey space with light. Today is the end of. I want to curl up in your Ercol chair. Can't seem to stop. I fuck you against the grey.

We share this same grey,
and I like this. I fuck you against the doorframe while the shadows watch.
Can't seem to stop. Today is Wednesday,
a grey Monday impersonator.
I want to curl up in your wool blanket.
Can't seem to stop thinking about this.
Shadows disappear, now we share the grey space with light.
Today is the end of.
I want to curl up in your Ercol chair.
Can't seem to stop.
I fuck you against the grey.

we share the same grey
we fuck against the doorframe
I can't seem to stop

Rollercoaster

i

I reach your summit, a white knuckle which pretends to be a hill. Your hand touches my hipbone, immediately I'm arms in air screaming, falling before I know it against the car door. My thighs become sticky like I'm on a synthetic seat masturbating whilst reading Anaïs Nin.

ii

I reach your summit, cry the initial of your name. I love this sound; it is as hollow as it is round. I'm diminuendo. I am heavy and sure as I fall. Downward Dog in reverse. I am light-fingered and circular. I am cross legged. I am in an egg swinging seat in the garden in July 40 degree, slowly falling asleep. I'm falling off a diving board before I'm ready. I'm head fucked, head rush in patterned dress, a neon paper bracelet from a night out in 96 around your fast-moving wrist.

iii

I reach your summit. My feet blur into your diminishing shadow while my hands become numb. I spot one of your *Converse* next to one of my *Louboutins* in the place where Manchester should be. Our shoes start a dance that was rehearsed once but not yet put into practice. My eyes are blurred from G force or orgasm, and this clouds my judgement. My stomach lands shortly after my feet, on a table reserved for bags to be searched. It makes a slapping sound as organs spill over the edge, I know it is mine, I recognise the scars.

Our Turn to Host

That the dinner party is ours is a bad start / I open the door / smile / take coats / observe new hair / enhanced romance between the couple we sit down with / every sentence I begin with I self-censor / make sure I'm not going to disclose too much / B notices but she's got the headfuck rush from the *Pata Negra* I bought at Madrid Airport / I'm struggling after two glasses of wine and 12 drops of rescue remedy / I want to smoke too fast / exhale this shit sham of an evening / At eight seventeen and we're one hour and sixteen minutes in / after melon and lamb and Hasselbach potatoes / here is the part when I want to cram soft sponge into my mouth like a gag / this is when B's husband asks about my job / I'm lying on the table naked / exposed as he dives in with precision / cuts into the decisions I make laid out on the table / dissecting me in parts / judging and measuring and weighing and labelling / I want to eat trifle and cry

Knife Fish

I'm writing to tell you it is 2.22am, I drank two coffees before I went to bed. I remember how you lift my dress slowly as if observing a Gursky photograph in The Hayward Gallery and I'm kneeling above you in a central display, the sign would read: **Woman, desire**, the words would describe nipples alive in a cadmium yellow illumination. Your smile does this, forty volts between cartilage and muscle, the way you look as my dress lowers, is electricity under my flesh. I'm all electrogenic tissue, I'm a Knife Fish in a French film.

Kefir

1. I am told to drink bacteria to help my gut, this will stop me being so fucked up.

2. I cannot survive without it.

3. I am led to believe my body is cruel, yet this will make me hungry again —

4. I think of peaches, tomatoes, I think of raspberries. I think of my lover.

5. My lover says my lips taste sour, a baby's bubbled breath, off milk.

6. I curdle under liquid which is blanket heavy.

7. I taste of drowning.

8. At sea, at sea, at sea.

9. I am sick, acid fragranced, drip-fed badness.

Acknowledgements

Thank you to the following publications who first published some of these poems: *Poetry Wales, Atrium, Northern Gravy, Dear Reader.*

Thank you to Aaron and Charlie for accepting this manuscript and supporting many writers who are starting out.

To the crew of the BA 456 flight. We had such fun. I loved flying with you all. The honesty of Cabin Crew influences everything I write.

To Richard Scott. Ella Frears, Julie Irigaray, Alycia Pirmohamed, Antony Dunn, Caroline Bird, and Rachel Long - I was so lucky to have been taught by you when I started writing.

Thank you to City Lit for their continued support of my work. Thank you to the Cheltenham Poetry Festival for running such important workshops and readings.

To Mary Jean Chan, Jenny Wong, Morag Joss, Niall Munro, The Brookes Poetry Centre and the de Rohan scholarship, thank you for everything you did for me while I studied at Oxford Brookes University. I loved being at Brookes.

To Galia Admoni, the Arvon Dreamers, Charley Barnes, Aidan Byrne, Lisa J Coates, Lucy Holme, Stuart McPherson, Ed Roffe, Antonia Taylor, and Laura Warner, thank you for your feedback and most importantly, your friendship.

To all the women who think they can't start again, you can.

LAY OUT YOUR UNREST